ENTERING
ROCKY MOUNTAIN
NATIONAL PARK

Images of
ROCKY MOUNTAIN
National Park

A photographic portfolio by
ERIK STENSLAND

Published by

Skyline Press

Post Office Box 371
Pueblo, Colorado 81002
www.skylinepress.com

ISBN: 978-1-888845-75-4
Photographs Copyright © Erik Stensland 2007

Base map courtesy National Park Service
Additional rendering by Michael Borop,
World Sites Atlas

Colorado
Souvenir
Series

COVER: Morning light at Sprague Lake
PREVIOUS PAGE: Sign post on Meadow Mountain
LEFT: Golden aspens below peaks of the Continental Divide
BACK COVER: Clouds fill Forest Canyon below Longs Peak

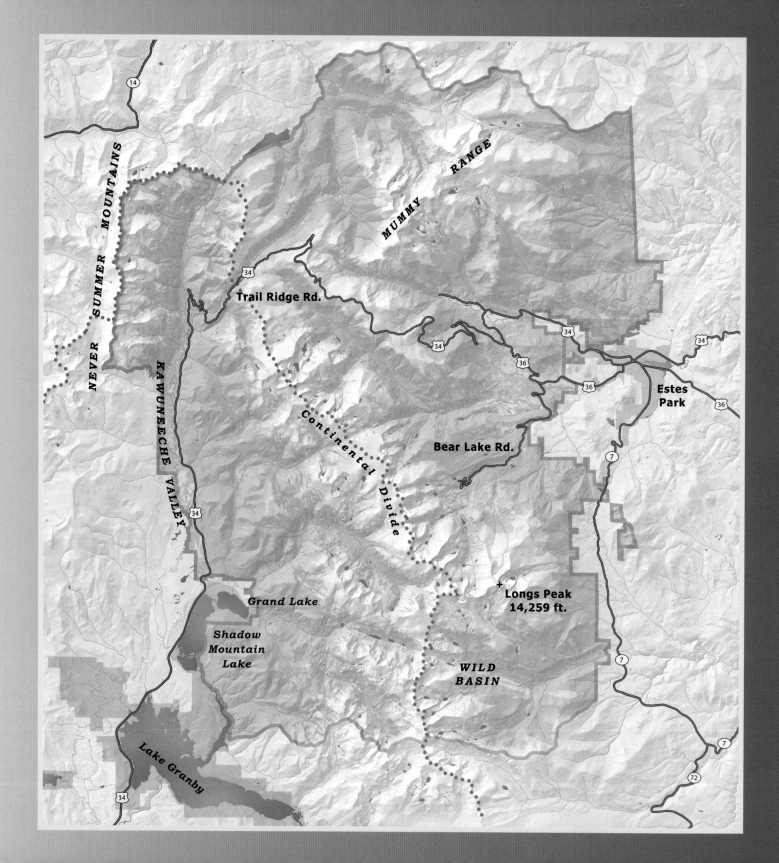

Introduction

The air is fresh and cool. A thousand stars shine brightly above me as I hike through open meadows and deep forests, hearing only the sound of my own breathing. It is calm, but I'm filled with expectation as I imagine what the dawn will bring. I arrive at a remote mountain lake just as the world begins to emerge under a strange blue hue. In minutes, the mountains begin to embrace a gentle, warming glow that gradually intensifies until they shine a deep red. The world explodes with color and my heart pounds with excitement as I struggle to capture something of this moment that is all too brief. While the drama unfolds before me, the forest begins to awaken. Birds begin to sing, and soon elk come out for a drink from the calm lake as a beaver takes his first swim of the new day. Something deep inside me wells up at the wonder of it all—it is in these special moments that I sense what it means to be alive.

We are made with a deep longing for beauty, and it is this longing that draws three million visitors to Rocky Mountain National Park each year. Within its compact 415 square miles, Rocky Mountain National Park contains nearly 150 mountain lakes, 450 miles of bubbling streams and 60 peaks over 12,000 feet high. The diversity of the park is breathtaking, and very few of those three million park visitors have taken the time to truly experience it.

Just beyond the main roads of the park lies a world of natural wonder and amazing beauty. Even on the busiest day of the year one can sit on the edge of a mountain lake, enjoy a stroll through tundra flowers or climb from peak to peak and never see another person. Rocky Mountain National Park offers serenity and beauty to those who seek it, while also enabling even those who are just passing through a chance to glimpse something of its wonder.

It is a place of diversity comprised of meadows and mountains, wetlands and tundra. The eastern side of the park lives up to the name "Rocky," beginning with the strange stone formations of Lumpy Ridge and stretching to the rugged mountains which rise to over 14,000'. In the west lie lush forests and the headwaters of the Colorado River, which eventually makes its way to the Grand Canyon and beyond. Between the two sides of the park is expansive alpine tundra with a delicate and unique ecosystem. Beyond these broad brush strokes, every valley of the park offers its own unique beauty, from waterfalls to hidden lakes and stunning views.

Rocky Mountain National Park is always changing. In late May the first flowers appear under the shade of the ponderosa pine forests. They migrate out into the fields, spreading their beauty and fragrance, slowly making their way up to the lakes and on to the tundra. Then, seemingly overnight, autumn arrives in the tundra with its rich reds and golds. It slowly works its way down to the valleys, setting the aspens alight in the most vibrant colors of yellow and orange. Soon, the winter snows create a new landscape of brilliant white under deep blue skies. Yet it isn't only the seasons which transform the park. Each day and hour, the sun highlights different aspects of the terrain. You can go back again and again to the same places but it is always different, ever-changing. It is an ongoing celebration of diversity and beauty.

The Onahu Trail winds through forests on the west side of Rocky Mountain National Park
FOLLOWING PAGES: Morning along the Big Thompson River, Moraine Park

Seasons collide on Twin Sisters Peaks
LEFT: Fresh snow and lone aspen tree, Horseshoe Park

Quiet calm on Lion Lake No. 1, Wild Basin
FACING PAGE: Little Matterhorn and Fern Creek near Odessa Lake

*L*ongs Peak is the true beacon of Rocky Mountain National Park. Rising to an elevation of 14,259 feet, its distinctive blocky summit can be seen from just about every point on a compass. It is the northernmost of Colorado's 54 fourteeners (peaks rising above 14,000 feet), making it the park's highest point. While it is viewed casually by anyone who visits Rocky—for instance, framed by the Rock Cut (FACING PAGE) on Trail Ridge Road—a few hundred hardy souls attempt to climb the peak on any given summer day. Striking out long before sunrise, climbers ascend the trail past such storied landmarks as the Boulderfield, the Keyhole (ABOVE), the Ledges, the Trough, the Narrows (those afraid of heights need not apply), and finally, the Homestretch, before topping out on Longs Peak's expansive summit. Many climbers wisely turn back when weather conditions, altitude sickness or lack of stamina become a factor, but for those who persevere on the 15-mile round-trip journey, it's a hard-won prize worth savoring. Those who attempt the climb will be following in the footsteps of surveyors from John Wesley Powell's expedition, who made the first recorded ascent of the mountain in 1868. While there is no written record of earlier climbs, it is believed that Native Americans probably preceded Powell's expedition to the summit. Longs Peak is named for explorer Major Stephen Long, who ventured into the area in the 1820s, but did not attempt to climb the peak.

Snow and ice patterns at Calypso Cascades, Wild Basin
LEFT: Fresh snow hides Copeland Lake in lower Wild Basin
FOLLOWING PAGES: Turning aspens and fresh snow in Horseshoe Park

Windswept trees frame peaks above The Loch in Loch Vale
FACING PAGE: Alberta Falls is one of the most popular hiking destinations in the park

The summer months bring a wide variety of wildflowers to Rocky Mountain National Park. Beginning in June, golden banner (FACING PAGE) begins to bloom in open meadows and among aspen forests in the park's lower elevations. As the temperature warms at higher elevations, species such as (ABOVE, LEFT TO RIGHT) Indian paintbrush and showy daisies, blue columbines (Colorado's state flower) and king's crown take up residence in alpine meadows and along noisy creeks. The wildflower season is all too brief, but beautiful while it lasts.

*E*lk are one of the most common large mammals encountered in Rocky Mountain National Park. Part of the deer family, they are second only to the moose in size. During summer months it is common to see large herds of elk grazing across the alpine tundra along Trail Ridge Road, where small traffic jams often occur as the animals lumber across the road. They seek the relative comfort of lower elevations during the cold winter months. Only male elk grow antlers—growth begins in the spring, protected by a soft covering called velvet through the summer. In late-summer the velvet begins to deteriorate and fall off, aided by the bull rubbing its antlers on any available foliage. During the mating season in the fall, called the rut, dominant bull elk keep close watch on their harems of females, fighting off lesser male challengers in violent skirmishes. It's during this time that it is most common to hear bull elk bugling, an unforgettable and unmistakable sound that echoes across the landscape for miles. Towards the end of winter the bull elk shed their antlers, and the process begins anew.

The dramatic façade of Ypsilon Mountain towers over Spectacle Lake in the Mummy Range

Approaching the Boulderfield provides a striking view of the Diamond on Longs Peak

Evening light at East Meadow, along the East Inlet Trail
RIGHT: Alpenglow sunrise over Moraine Park and the Big Thompson River

Ptarmigan Mountain reflects in Lake Nanita in the remote western region of the park

Wildflowers and waterfalls below the Cleaver, East Inlet
FOLLOWING PAGES: Peaks of the Continental Divide reflect in Bierstadt Lake

Calypso Cascades tumbles through the forest in Wild Basin

A leaf-catcher pine tree holds fallen aspen leaves above Endovalley
RIGHT: Expansive Moraine Park welcomes the arrival of fall

Wind-whipped snow swirls around Flattop Mountain's many spires
LEFT: Two Rivers Lake thaws to reflect Notchtop Mountain

A dramatic view of Longs Peak from just below the Keyhole

Morning clouds spill over Hallett Peak and Flattop Mountain above Dream Lake

The rising sun brings a warm glow to an icy pond below Longs Peak
FACING PAGE: The eastern sky reflects its brilliant sunrise colors on Bear Lake's frozen surface

Fallen aspen leaves frame Boulder Brook
LEFT: The Never Summer Mountains form the backdrop to
the Kawuneeche Valley, prime elk and moose habitat on the park's west side

Indian paintbrush and elephanthead wildflowers proliferate on the shore of Bluebird Lake, Wild Basin

Chasm Falls is a must-see stop along Old Fall River Road

Trail Ridge Road (RIGHT), reaches nearly 12,200 feet at its highest point, making it the highest continuous paved road in the United States. Usually open from Memorial Day to the first substantial snows in mid-October, it provides unparalleled views of Longs Peak, and in summer its higher reaches play host to large herds of elk trying to escape the heat of the lower elevations. Entering the park on its east side at the Fall River entrance, the road climbs to timberline at Rainbow Curve, continues across alpine tundra, and drops back into the trees just below Medicine Bow Curve. Trail Ridge Road crosses the Continental Divide at 10,758-foot Milner Pass before dropping into the expansive Kawuneeche Valley on the park's west side.

Lake Verna reflects sunset light deep in the heart of the park's western interior
FACING PAGE: Sunrise at Solitude Lake, a remote alpine gem high above Glacier Gorge
FOLLOWING PAGES: Morning fog fills valleys of Glacier Basin

A beautiful summer day at
Thunder Lake, Wild Basin
FACING PAGE: Mount Julian and Cracktop
rise above Arrowhead Lake in the
remote Gorge Lakes area

Outstretched arms of an aspen tree above Hollowell Park

FACING PAGE: Autumn aspens surround Bear Lake as the day's last rays light Longs Peak and Keyboard of the Winds

Spirit Lake reflection in the Upper East Inlet

A peaceful morning below Gabletop Mountain

Rocky Mountain National Park is home to a diverse and abundant wildlife population,
including (CLOCKWISE FROM LEFT) bighorn sheep, bobcats, ground squirrels and marmots
FOLLOWING PAGES: The aftermath of a winter storm in the Mummy Range

The Diamond, Longs Peak's dramatic east face, rises above Chasm Lake

Hallett Peak reflects in the rock-strewn waters of Lake Haiyaha

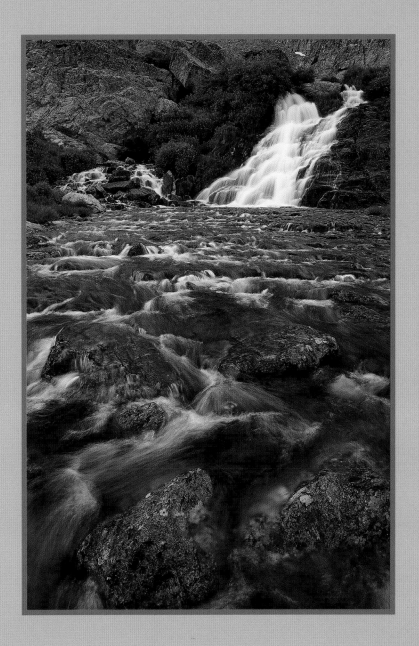

A waterfall near Sky Pond, high in Loch Vale
LEFT: The Nokhu Crags create an impressive skyline from Forest Canyon Pass

Lily pads and fog at Ouzel Lake, Wild Basin
FACING PAGE: Longs Peak rises high over Beaver Meadows

Photo by Michael Hodges

About the Photographer

*E*rik Stensland was born in 1968 in Minneapolis, Minnesota. He soon moved to Montana where he developed a deep love for the mountains. From a very early age he was hiking and exploring the streams and forests around his mountain home.

In 1978 Erik's family returned to Minnesota where he completed his early education. In 1991 after finishing college, he moved to Europe where he met his wife Joanna. They married and moved to Albania and later Kosovo, where they spent a decade assisting local churches and development agencies. In January 2004, they returned to the States so that Erik could complete his MA in Organizational Development.

They settled near Rocky Mountain National Park in Colorado which enabled Erik to pursue his love of nature through photography. With the beauty of Rocky Mountain National Park literally at his doorstep, Erik frequently rises long before dawn to hike to remote lakes or up high peaks to capture the unparalleled beauty of the park in warm morning light. His work has been featured in dozens of art shows, in the Colorado State Capitol rotunda and in numerous galleries.

All of the images in this book are available for purchase as fine art prints. To learn more about Erik and his photography, visit his Web site at:

www.imagesofRMNP.com